St. Thomas
the Apostle

Martyr

Prayer Journal

"Didymus"

Feast Day
3 July

Cover Photo Source: Wikimedia Commons user Andreas F. Borchert
Used under the Creative Commons Attribution-Share Alike 4.0 International license.

ISBN 978-1-716-48703-3
©2020 Catholic Treehouse

"But he who was now the most weak and unbelieving of all the disciples, afterwards became stronger than any. And he who dared not go to Bethany, afterwards went over the whole earth, in the midst of those who wished his death, with a spirit indomitable."

ST. JOHN CHRYSOSTOM

The Incredulity of Saint Thomas
by Michelangelo Merisi da Caravaggio

Biography of St. Thomas the Apostle

Little is recorded of St. Thomas the Apostle, nevertheless thanks to the fourth Gospel his personality is clearer to us than that of some others of the Twelve. His name occurs in all the lists of the Synoptists (Matthew 10:3; Mark 3:18; Luke 6, cf. Acts 1:13), but in St. John he plays a distinctive part. First, when Jesus announced His intention of returning to Judea to visit Lazarus, "Thomas" who is called Didymus [the twin], said to his fellow disciples: "Let us also go, that we may die with him" (John 11:16). Again it was St. Thomas who during the discourse before the Last Supper raised an objection: "Thomas saith to him: Lord, we know not whither thou goest; and how can we know the way?" (John 14:5). But more especially St. Thomas is remembered for his incredulity when the other Apostles announced Christ's Resurrection to him: "Except I shall see in his hands the print of the nails, and put my finger into the place of the nails, and put my hand into his side, I will not believe" (John 20:25); but eight days later he made his act of faith, drawing down the rebuke of Jesus: "Because thou hast seen me, Thomas, thou hast believed; blessed are they that have not seen, and have believed" (John 20:29).

This exhausts all our certain knowledge regarding the Apostle but his name is the starting point of a considerable apocryphal literature, and there are also certain historical data which suggest that some of this apocryphal material may contains germs of truth. The principal document concerning him is the "Acta Thomae", preserved to us with some variations both in Greek and in Syriac, and bearing unmistakeable signs of its Gnostic origin. It may indeed be the work of Bardesanes himself. The story in many of its particulars is utterly extravagant, but it is the early date, being assigned by Harnack (Chronologie, ii, 172) to the beginning of the third century, before A.D. 220. If the place of its origin is really Edessa, as Harnack and others for sound reasons supposed (ibid., p. 176), this would lend considerable probability to the statement, explicitly made in "Acta" (Bonnet, cap. 170, p. 286), that the relics of Apostle Thomas, which we know to have been venerated at Edessa, had really come from the East. The extravagance of the legend may be judged from the fact that in more than one place (cap. 31, p. 148) it represents Thomas (Judas Thomas, as he is called here and elsewhere in Syriac tradition) as the twin brother of Jesus. The Thomas in Syriac is equivalent to *didymos* in Greek, and means twin. Rendel Harris who exaggerates very much the cult of the Dioscuri, wishes to regards this as a transformation of a pagan worship of Edessa but the point is at best problematical. The story itself runs briefly as follows: At the division of the Apostles, India fell to the lot of Thomas, but he declared his inability to go, whereupon his Master Jesus appeared in a supernatural way to Abban, the envoy of Gundafor, an Indian king, and sold Thomas to him to be his slave and serve Gundafor as a carpenter. Then Abban and Thomas sailed away until they came to Andrapolis, where they landed and attended the marriage feast of the ruler's daughter. Strange occurrences followed and Christ under the appearance of Thomas exhorted the bride to remain a Virgin. Coming to India Thomas undertook to build a palace for Gundafor, but spend the money entrusted to him on the poor. Gundafor imprisoned him; but the Apostle escaped miraculously and Gundafor was converted. Going about the country to preach, Thomas met with strange adventures from dragons and wild asses. Then he came to the city of King Misdai (Syriac Mazdai), where he converted Tertia the wife of Misdai and Vazan his son. After this he was condemned to death, led out of city to a hill, and pierced through with spears by four soldiers. He was buried in the tomb of the ancient kings but his remains were afterwards removed to the West.

Now it is certainly a remarkable fact that about the year A.D. 46 a king was reigning over that part of Asia south of Himalayas now represented by Afghanistan, Baluchistan, the Punjab, and Sind, who bore the name Gondophernes or Guduphara. This we know both from the discovery of coins, some of the Parthian type with Greek legends, others of the Indian types with the legends in an Indian dialect in Kharoshthi characters. Despite sundry minor variations the identity of the name with the Gundafor of the "Acta Thomae" is unmistakable and is hardly disputed. Further we have the evidence of the Takht-i-Bahi inscription, which is dated and which the best specialists accept as establishing the King Gunduphara probably began to reign about A.D. 20 and was still reigning in 46. Again there are excellent reasons for believing that Misdai or Mazdai may well be transformation of a Hindu name made on the Iranian soil. In this case it will probably represent a certain King Vasudeva of Mathura, a successor of Kanishka. No doubt it can be urged that the Gnostic romancer who wrote the "Acta Thomae" may have adopted a few historical Indian names to lend verisimilitude to his fabrication, but as Mr. Fleet urges in his severely critical paper "the names put forward here in connection with St.Thomas are distinctly not such as have lived in Indian story and tradition" (Journal of R. Asiatic Soc., 1905, p. 235).

On the other hand, though the tradition that St. Thomas preached in "India" was widely spread in both East and West and is to be found in such writers as Ephraem Syrus, Ambrose, Paulinus, Jerome, and, later Gregory of Tours and others, still it is difficult to discover any adequate support for the long-accepted belief that St. Thomas pushed his missionary journeys as far south as Mylapore, not far from Madras, and there suffered martyrdom. In that region is still to be found a granite bas-relief cross with a Pahlavi (ancient Persian) inscription dating from the seventh century, and the tradition that it was here that St. Thomas laid down his life is locally very strong.

Certain it is also that on the Malabar or west coast of southern India a body of Christians still exists using a form of Syriac for its liturgical language. Whether this Church dates from the time of St. Thomas the Apostle (there was a Syro-Chaldean bishop John "from India and Persia" who assisted at the Council of Nicea in 325) or whether the Gospel was first preached there in 345 owing to the Persian persecution under Shapur (or Sapor), or whether the Syrian missionaries who accompanied a certain Thomas Cana penetrated to the Malabar coast about the year 745 seems difficult to determine. We know only that in the sixth century Cosmas Indicopleustes speaks of the existence of Christians at Male (perhaps Malabar) under a bishop who had been consecrated in Persia. King Alfred the Great is stated in the "Anglo-Saxon Chronicle" to have sent an expedition to establish relations with these Christians of the Far East. On the other hand the reputed relics of St. Thomas were certainly at Edessa in the fourth century, and there they remained until they were translated to Chios in 1258 and towards to Ortona. The improbable suggestion that St. Thomas preached in America (American Eccles. Rev., 1899, pp. 1-18) is based upon a misunderstanding of the text of the Acts of the Apostles (1:8; cf. Berchet "Fonte italiane per la storia della scoperta del Nuovo Mondo", II, 236, and I, 44).

Besides the "Acta Thomae" of which a different and notably shorter redaction exists in Ethiopic and Latin, we have an abbreviated form of a so-called "Gospel of Thomas" originally Gnostic, as we know it now merely a fantastical history of the childhood of Jesus, without any notably heretical coloring. There is also a "Revelatio Thomae," condemned as apocryphal in the Decree of Pope Gelasius, which has recently been recovered from various sources in a fragmentary condition (see the full text in the Revue benedictine, 1911, pp. 359-374).

CITATION: Thurston, H. (1912). St. Thomas the Apostle. In *The Catholic Encyclopedia*. New York: Robert Appleton Company. Retrieved October 20, 2020 from New Advent: *http://www.newadvent.org/cathen/14658b.htm*

TOMAS

St. Thomas the Apostle
by Father Francis Xavier Weninger, 1876

St. Thomas was a fisherman, born in Galilee. The divine Savior received him among His Apostles, to announce His Gospel to the world, and to convert mankind. From the time that he was chosen to so high an office, Thomas followed his beloved Master everywhere, and feared no danger. One day, when Jesus spoke of going to Judaea, to awaken Lazarus from the dead, some of His disciples opposed Him, saying: "Rabbi, the Jews but now sought to stone Thee, and goest Thou to that place again?" They probably feared that they would have to suffer with Him. Thomas, however, more courageous than the others, said: "Let us also go, that we may die with Him." By these words the Apostle manifested that no fear of death would separate him from Christ; and that, rather than leave Him, he would die with Him. It is true that later, with other disciples, he left Him on the Mount of Olives, when He was taken prisoner by the Jews; but he returned soon, and joined the rest of the Apostles.

On the day of His resurrection, Christ appeared to them. Thomas, however, was not with them. When they told him afterwards, that they had seen the Lord, he doubted, and said: "Except I shall see in His hands the print of the nails, and put my finger into the place of the nails, and put my hand into His side, I will not believe." By this, Thomas meant that he did not believe the resurrection of the Lord, although he had several times heard from the lips of Jesus, not only a prophecy of His sufferings and death, but also of His resurrection; and although the Apostles and several pious women had repeatedly assured him that they had seen the risen Lord. The Holy Fathers say that Christ permitted this unbelief in Thomas, not only that from it we might learn our own weakness, but also that all who believe in Him might be so much better instructed in the mystery of His resurrection, and strengthened in their belief in it. Hence, St. Gregory writes: "The unbelief of Thomas has been more useful to our belief than the belief of the other disciples of the Lord, who, without hesitation, received the news of His resurrection," because the unbelief of Thomas gave occasion for new proofs of the resurrection of Christ.

The eighth day after that event, Christ came into the hall where Thomas was with the other Apostles, and greeted them with the words: "Peace be unto you." Then, turning to Thomas, He said: "Put in thy finger hither, and see my hands; and reach hither thy hand, and put it into my side; and be not faithless, but believing." What Thomas must have felt at these words, and at seeing his risen Savior, each one may picture to himself. He saw himself suddenly convinced, not only of the resurrection, but also of the omniscience of his dear Master. With shame and fear at the remembrance of his fault, but also with love and confidence at the thought of the meekness of the Savior, he touched, with deep veneration, the holy wounds, and exclaimed: "My Lord and my God!" In these few words he repented of his unbelief, and at the same time made a confession of his faith, in presence of those whom he had scandalized by his obstinacy. He remained until his end, constant in his belief; and, after the descent of the Holy Ghost, announced, not only the glorious resurrection of the Lord, but also the other mysteries and articles of the faith.

St. Thomas passed some time in Judaea, preaching the Gospel, and then went into distant countries, inhabited by savage races, as Parthia, Media, Persia, Hyrcania, and came, at last, to India. In all he preached the Gospel of the Lord, notwithstanding the manifold difficulties which the Evil One placed in his way, through the enemies of the faith, and the numerous persecutions which he everywhere endured. How many thousand souls this holy Apostle converted to Christ is known only to Him from whom nothing is hid. The many miracles which he almost daily performed, persuaded the people that the faith which he preached was truly divine: hence his success with the most embittered pagans. He made the largest number of converts in India. This immense territory he traversed in every direction, and established Christianity in it so firmly, that traces of it were found there in the sixteenth century, fifteen hundred years after his death. Even in China, indubitable signs of it were discovered. He erected many churches, and placed Christian teachers in them, that the faith he had personally preached during his life might be preserved after his death.

At the building of the church at Meliapor, one of the chief cities of India, a wonderful event took place. The sea had cast ashore a very large tree, which the king desired to make use of for the palace he was just erecting. But neither men nor many elephants could move the tree. The holy Apostle, full of trust in the Almighty, offered to draw the immense burden all alone, if the king would make him a present of it for the Christian church he was about to build. The king consented, and St. Thomas, loosening his girdle, tied the end of it to one branch of the tree, made the sign of the Cross, and drew the tree away from the place where it was lying. All present were greatly astonished at this miracle, and many were converted, and assisted the Apostle in building the church. In this church the Saint erected a cross of stone, which, it is said, is still to be seen at this day. Upon this cross he engraved the following words: "When the sea will have reached this spot, men will come from Europe to propagate the faith which I began to preach." The sea was, at that time, far off, but at the time when St. Francis Xavier landed there, it had reached the cross, and the prophecy was fulfilled.

The idolatrous priests who could not contradict the faith which St. Thomas preached, and which he verified by so many miracles, were enraged at his success, as they lost considerably in temporal goods by the conversions that took place. They therefore endeavored to arouse the king's wrath against him, or to make away with him in some other manner. Some write that they persuaded the king to pronounce his death-sentence, and that he was shot dead with arrows. Others relate that the Brahmins themselves took the life of the holy Apostle. They had ascertained that the Saint went every day, towards evening, to a cross which he himself had erected, and that he remained there a long time in prayer. This gave them a favorable opportunity to vent their wrath upon him. They came together silently to the place where, on bended knees, the Saint was saying his prayers. One of them thrust a lance into him so violently that he sank upon the ground; after which, the others continued to beat him and to trample on him until all signs of life ceased.

When St. Francis Xavier came to India, the signs of blood were still to be seen on the cross where this murderous deed was committed; and more than once drops of blood appeared on this cross during the celebration of Mass, when crowds of people were present. St. Xavier, shortly after his arrival in India, went to the tomb of St. Thomas, and passed many days and nights there in prayer. He begged God fervently to bestow upon him the Spirit and zeal of this holy Apostle, that he might be able to restore the Christian faith which St. Thomas had preached there, but which had gradually been entirely exterminated. Before undertaking any important work, he went, if possible, to the tomb of St. Thomas; and when this was impossible, he invoked the holy Apostle's intercession, and endeavored to follow his example in all things.

Practical Considerations

I. St. Thomas, for three years, accompanied Christ our Lord; was present at His divine instructions; saw the many miracles He wrought; and yet became incredulous and remained so for eight days, and might have remained still longer, had not Christ mercifully restored his faith. Go, O man, and build upon your own strength, or if you have lived piously for some time, imagine you are secure against falling! Oh! how foolish, how presumptuous you are! That which happened to an apostle may surely happen to you. The sad fall of our holy Apostle, ought not, however, to make you despondent or fearful; it ought only to incite you not to trust too much in your own strength, but to walk continually in the fear of the Lord, and to pray to Him daily, that He may give you the grace not to offend Him, but to remain constant in His service If you remain continually in the fear of the Lord, you will walk carefully and not fall into any great sin. For, it is written: "The fear of the Lord is unto life; and he shall abide in fulness without being visited with evil," (without falling into sin.) (Proverbs, xix.) Tertullian writes: "Fear is the foundation of our salvation. Whoever fears is careful. Through fear we shall become careful, and through carefulness we shall be saved.

Whoever is careful is sure." If we cease to fear God, then we are near falling, even if we have reached the highest pinnacle of perfection. This the Holy Ghost indicates in the following words: "Unless thou hold thyself diligently in the fear of the Lord, thy house shall quickly be overthrown." (Eccles. 27.)

II. Thomas is called unbelieving by Christ, although he disbelieved only one article, the resurrection. Hence, it is clear that he who doubts, or rejects only one article of faith, cannot be counted among true Catholics, although he believes all the others. A Catholic must believe every truth revealed by the Almighty, be it great or small, as God cannot fail either in small things or great. The offense which we do to God by denying even the smallest article of faith, is as great as if we denied an important one, or all of them together; for, it is just as if we said: God has been deceived, or He has deceived us in revealing this article. Whether this is said of great and important articles, or of one that is small, makes but little difference; or if we desire to make a difference, we must say that it is a greater offense to God to ascribe to Him a fault in a small matter than in a great; for, what can be more blasphemous than to maintain that the Almighty has been deceived in a trifling matter, or that He intends to deceive us? They should ponder on this, who sometimes entertain doubts about an article of faith, or even go so far as to say that in some matters, they agree with non-Catholics, and consider them right. These are no longer Catholics. Their faith is lost; and if they do not repent, as St. Thomas did, they will go to perdition, because they are incredulous. They are disobedient who obey nine of the Commandments but not the tenth. What is the fate of the incredulous? Christ Himself pointed it out when He said: "Who believes not in the Son, will not see life, but the wrath of God will remain with him." (John 8)

"Thomas saith to him: Lord, we know not whither thou goest. And how can we know the way? Jesus saith to him: I am the way, and the truth, and the life. No man cometh to the Father, but by me."

John 14:5-6

"**Let us also go, that we may die with Him.**" Not with Lazarus, as some will have it, for this seems foolish; but with Christ, who a little before had said, "Let us go to him." Thomas exhorts his companions beyond all, that they should go and die with Christ, in which his great constancy appears. Behold the true disposition of loving souls, either to live with Him or to die with Him... that which St. Thomas says, "Let us also go, that we may die with Him," is as if he had said, "If we go with Jesus, we must die with Him, because of the violent hatred of the Jews towards Him. If then He goes, let us also go, as brave disciples and soldiers, and die with Him courageously as our Leader; if He disregards death, and even advances to meet it, let us also disregard it and meet it." ... Therefore he offers himself for Christ to certain death, for he considered it was impending; which was a remarkable proof of his great bravery, and singular love for Christ.

FROM THE GREAT BIBLICAL COMMENTARY OF CORNELIUS À LAPIDE

Novena to St. Thomas the Apostle

Lord Jesus, Saint Thomas doubted Your resurrection until he touched Your wounds. After Pentecost, You called him to become a missionary in India but he doubted again and said no. He changed his mind only after being taken into slavery by a merchant who happened to be going to India. Once he was cured of his doubt, You freed him and he began the work You had called him to do. As the Patron Saint against Doubt, I ask him to pray for me when I question the direction in which You are leading me. Forgive me for mistrusting You, Lord, and help me to grow from the experience.

Saint Thomas the Apostle, *pray for me.* Amen.

Almighty and ever-living God, who didst strengthen thine apostle Thomas with sure and certain faith in thy Son's resurrection:

Grant us so perfectly and without doubt to believe in Jesus Christ, our Lord and our God, that our faith may never be found wanting in thy sight, through him who liveth and reigneth with thee and the Holy Spirit, one God, now and forever.

It is through the intercession of holy St. Thomas the Apostle that we raise to Thee the following petition: *(State your intention.)*

(One Our Father, one Hail Mary, one Glory Be.)

Saint Thomas the Apostle, *pray for us!* Amen

DESCENDIT AD INFEROS TERTIA DIE RESURREXIT A MORTUIS

Impij Apollinis sacerdotes in Thomam cuius sera irruunt ac Pennson primis gladiis Aplm transfodit.

Recognosci fili cogitatio in ara deorum fornicem Thomae rumpit qui postridie integer surgit.

S. THOMAS APLVS

Æ.F. Rem Nicolai Van Aelst fe.

Prayers to St. Thomas the Apostle

Prayer to St. Thomas the Apostle for Faith (Long)

O GLORIOUS APOSTLE THOMAS, who didst lead to Christ so many unbelieving nations, hear now the prayers of the faithful, who beseech thee to lead them to that same Jesus, Who, in five days, will have shown Himself to His Church. That we may merit to appear in His divine presence, we need, before all other graces, the light which leads to Him. That light is Faith; then, pray that we may have Faith. Heretofore, our Savior had compassion on thy weakness, and deigned to remove from thee the doubt of His having risen from the grave; pray to Him for us, that He will mercifully come to our assistance, and make Himself felt by our heart. We ask not, O holy Apostle! to see Him with the eyes of our body, but with those of our faith, for He said to thee, when He showed himself to thee: Blessed are they who have not seen, and have believed!

Of this happy number, we desire to be. We beseech thee, therefore, pray that we may obtain the Faith of the heart and will, that so, when we behold the divine Infant wrapped in swaddling-clothes and laid in a manger, we may cry out: My Lord! and my God! Pray, O holy Apostle, for the nations thou didst evangelize, but which have fallen back again into the shades of death. May the day soon come, when the Sun of Justice will once more shine upon them. Bless the efforts of those apostolic men, who have devoted their labors and their very lives to the work of the Missions; pray that the days of darkness may be shortened, and that the countries, which were watered by thy blood, may at length see that kingdom of God established amongst them, which thou didst preach to them, and for which we also are in waiting.

Prayer to St. Thomas the Apostle for Faith (Short)

ALMIGHTY AND EVER LIVING GOD, who didst strengthen thine apostle Thomas with sure and certain faith in thy Son's resurrection: Grant us so perfectly and without doubt to believe in Jesus Christ, our Lord and our God, that our faith may never be found wanting in thy sight; through him who liveth and reigneth with thee and the Holy Spirit, one God, now and for ever. Amen.

Prayer for Committing Ourselves to God's Service
O Glorious Saint Thomas, your grief for Jesus was such that it would not let you believe He had risen unless you actually saw Him and touched His wounds. But your love for Jesus was equally great and it led you to give up your life for Him. Pray for us that we may grieve for our sins which were the cause of Christ's sufferings. Help us to give ourselves in His service and so earn the title of "blessed" which Jesus applied to those who would believe in Him without seeing Him. Amen.

Prayer for the Intercession of St. Thomas
Lord Jesus, St. Thomas doubted Your resurrection until he touched Your wounds. After Pentecost, You called him to become a missionary in India, but he doubted again and said no. He changed his mind only after being taken into slavery by a merchant who happened to be going to India. Once he was cured of his doubt, You freed him and he began the work You had called him to do. As the patron saint against doubt, I ask him to pray for me when I question the direction in which You are leading me. Forgive me for mistrusting You, Lord, and help me to grow from the experience. Saint Thomas, pray for me. Amen.

Prayer for Architects, Builders and Carpenters
Dear St. Thomas, you were once slow in believing that Christ had gloriously risen; but later, because you had seen him, you exclaimed: "My Lord and my God!" According to an ancient story, you rendered most powerful assistance for constructing a church in a place where pagan priests opposed it. Please bless architects, builders, and carpenters that through them the Lord may be honored. Amen.

Collect Prayer for St. Thomas the Apostle
Everliving God, who strengthened your apostle Thomas with firm and certain faith in your Son's resurrection: Grant us so perfectly and without doubt to believe in Jesus Christ, our Lord and our God, that our faith may never be found wanting in your sight; through him who lives and reigns with you and the Holy Spirit, one God, now and for ever. Amen

Feast Day Prayer for St. Thomas the Apostle
Almighty Father, as we honor Thomas the apostle, let us always experience the help of his prayers. May we have eternal life by believing in Jesus, whom Thomas acknowledged as Lord who lives and reigns with you in the unity of the Holy Spirit, one God, forever and ever. Amen

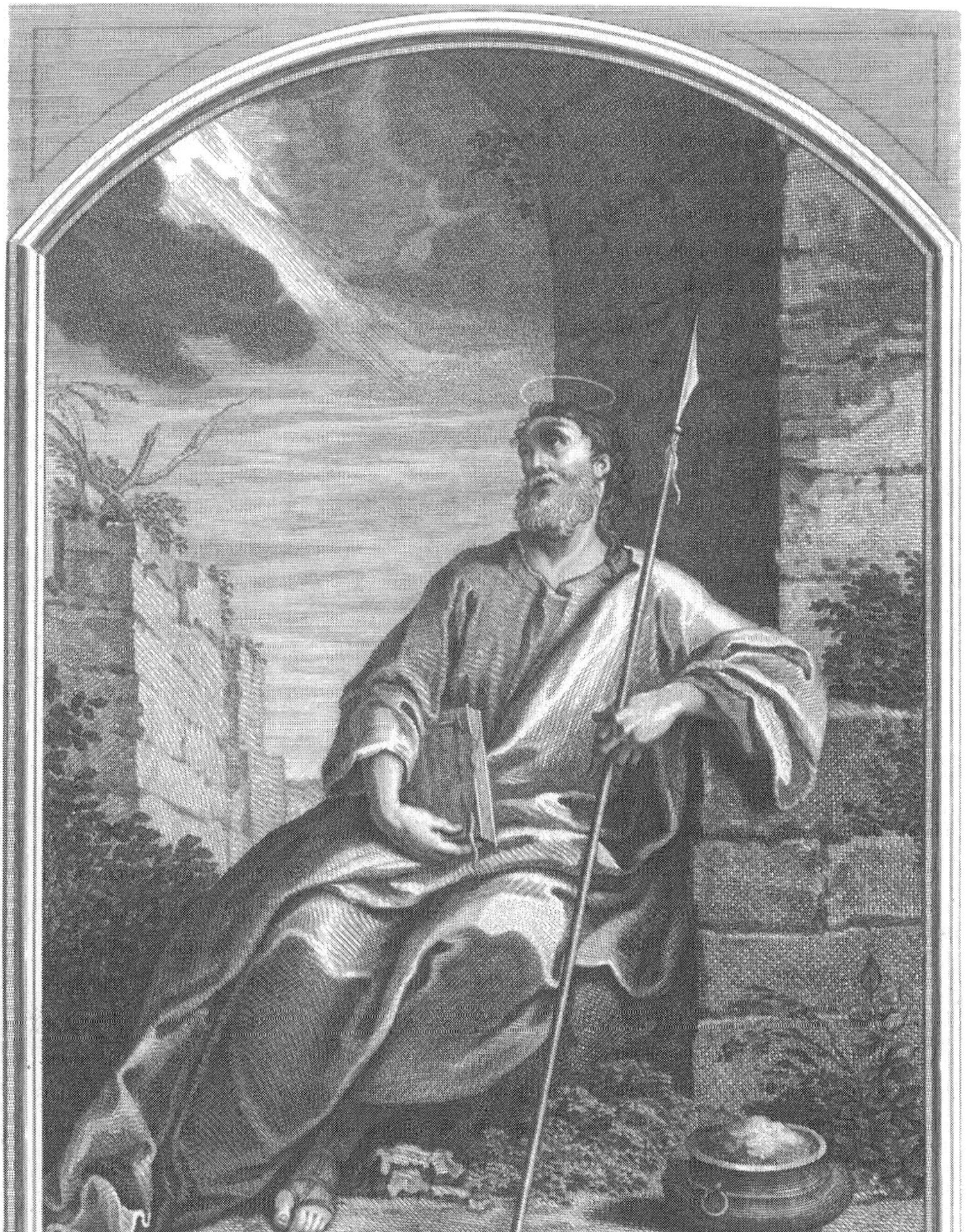

"Jesus saith to him: Because thou hast seen me, Thomas, thou hast believed: blessed are they that have not seen and have believed."

John 20:29

Prayer Journal

Made in the USA
Middletown, DE
14 April 2022